COLLEGE FOOTBALL >> SEASON TICKET

THE ULTIMATE FAN GUIDE

D1715325

BY DAVE CAMPBELL

First Edition
First Printing, 2019

Book design by Sarah Taplin
Cover design by Sarah Taplin
Photographs ©: The Tournament of Roses/AP Images, cover (top); Jae C. Hong/AP Images, cover (left); David Goldman/AP Images, cover (center right); Scott Stuart/Cal Sport Media/AP Images, cover (bottom right); Ray Carlin/Icon Sportswire, 4, 15; Reed Saxon/ AP Images, 9; Chris Carlson/AP Images, 11; North Wind Picture Archives/AP Images, 16; AP Images, 22–23, 24, 28, 34, 39, 40, 43, 57, 60; Mark Lambie/AP Images, 31; Doug Murray/ Icon Sportswire, 33; Carl Viti/AP Images, 44; Patrick S. Blood/Icon Sportswire, 49; Carlos Osorio/AP Images, 51; Dave Martin/AP Images, 53, 54; Pro Football Hall of Fame/AP Images, 62–63; Tom DiPace/AP Images, 64; Debby Wong/Shutterstock Images, 66; Jack Harris/AP Images, 70; Chris O'Meara/AP Images, 72–73; Eric Gay/AP Images, 74; Steve Nurenberg/ Icon Sportswire, 79; Anthony Souffle/Star Tribune/AP Images, 80–81; Elaine Thompson/AP Images, 82; Austin McAfee/Cal Sport Media/AP Images, 86–87; Matt Slocum/AP Images, 89; Todd Kirkland/Icon Sportswire, 90; John Bazemore/AP Images, 95

Design Elements ©: Pixabay

Press Box Books, an imprint of Press Room Editions.

Library of Congress Control Number: 2018952206

ISBN:
978-1-63494-056-6 (paperback)
978-1-63494-068-9 (epub)
978-1-63494-080-1 (hosted ebook)

Distributed by North Star Editions, Inc.
2297 Waters Drive
Mendota Heights, MN 55120
www.northstareditions.com

Printed in the United States of America

TABLE OF CONTENTS

CHAPTER 1

THE PLAYOFF AT LAST

Confetti fluttered down from the Dallas Cowboys' stadium. Cardale Jones had just received a postgame hug from one of Ohio State's most famous fans, basketball star LeBron James. Now Jones and his teammates danced on a makeshift stage. The night of January 12, 2015, was one they'd remember forever. The Buckeyes had beaten the Oregon Ducks to claim college football's national championship.

Of all the forms of entertainment, sports have long stood as the strong favorite. Highly anticipated games can fill stadiums with more than 100,000 screaming fans. TV audiences can reach tens of millions.

 Quarterback Cardale Jones celebrates Ohio State's historic national title on January 12, 2015.

We marvel at the agility, speed, and strength of the athletes. We're captivated by the unpredictable drama that can unfold during any given game. There's the unmistakable allure, too, of the intensity and tension that surrounds any competition.

But what if we weren't sure exactly who the winner was?

That used to be an issue for major college football. Until the 2014 season, when Ohio State beat Oregon to win the first College Football Playoff, the sport crowned a champion in a unique—and often frustrating—way.

Top-level college football teams are based all around the country. There's no way every team can play all the others during the regular season. So the sport long ago turned to opinion polls. Instead of settling the score on the field, coaches or sports reporters voted to determine the best team. Whoever received the most votes was named national champion.

Of course, this system could never last, right? In fact it did, for many decades. One reason for this was bowl games. These iconic postseason games, such as the Rose Bowl and Orange Bowl, have long histories of their own. Teams with winning records are invited to participate. Some bowl games have a great deal of prestige and tradition. For example, winning the Big Ten Conference and earning a berth in the Rose Bowl was—and still is—a big deal. Bowl games also brought in a lot of money to the schools.

However, this bowl system meant there was no guarantee that the best two teams would meet on the field. That's where the polls came in.

In many years, polls did produce a clear national champion. The Associated Press (AP) writers' poll, which was created in 1936, often agreed with the coaches' poll and crowned the same team. However, the system also had its share of flaws.

For example, the two main polls didn't always agree. When this happened, two teams ended the season claiming they were national champion. Another problem was that, until 1969, the final rankings were released before the bowl games. Several times, a team finished the regular season ranked No. 1 only to lose a bowl game, yet that team was still considered the national champ. And then there was the issue of perception. Was an undefeated team in a weaker conference more deserving than a one-loss team from a power conference? Only the voters could decide.

The controversy increased through the years to the point where Congress became involved. It held hearings to examine what many believed was a broken system.

The 1990 season highlighted the challenges. Georgia Tech finished 11–0–1 after beating Nebraska decisively in the Citrus Bowl. Colorado defeated Notre Dame in the Orange Bowl to go 11–1–1. However, the Buffaloes' season included a controversial win over Missouri in which they were mistakenly allowed a fifth down to keep a last-minute game-winning drive going. In the end, Georgia Tech topped the coaches' poll by an 847–846 margin over Colorado. But Colorado took the AP poll honor. Others yet argued for Miami as the best team that season.

A similar situation arose the next year. The most dominant Washington team in program history went undefeated, winning the coaches' vote. But Miami prevailed in the AP poll despite having one loss.

Then, in 1997, Michigan and Nebraska led the way all season, but they never met on the field. Because the Rose Bowl was long tied to the Big Ten, Michigan played its bowl game there. The Orange Bowl had a tie-in to the Big 12 Conference, where Nebraska

Michigan's Jerame Tuman hauls in a touchdown pass in the Rose Bowl on January 1, 1998.

played, so the Huskers went there. When both teams won their bowl games, the writers favored Michigan and the coaches voted for Nebraska.

It was time for a change. The Bowl Championship Series (BCS), created in 1998, aimed to do just that. In this system, the BCS combined polls with other factors to rank the teams. Four major bowl games partnered with the BCS, and one agreed each year to host a

1-vs.-2 matchup, regardless of conference affiliation. This ensured there would be a true title game.

The BCS model still had flaws. In 2003, the top three teams each had one loss going into the bowl games, but only two could play each other for the BCS title. So when the dust settled, both Louisiana State University (LSU) and Southern Cal (USC) won their bowl games and claimed bragging rights. The same thing happened in 2004. Auburn went unbeaten. So did USC and Oklahoma, which played for the BCS championship in the Orange Bowl. Auburn's win over Virginia Tech in the Sugar Bowl gave the Tigers a 13–0 record, but technically not the national title. Coach Tommy Tuberville turned reflective in his postgame address to his proud but disappointed players.

"You guys started something tonight that will change college football," Tuberville told the team, as he recounted later to ESPN.com. "It's going to take five, 10, 15, 20 years, but because of what this group did, went undefeated, it opened the eyes of people across the country."

Originally, one of the four BCS bowl games each year was designated as the national title game. Starting in the 2006 season, the BCS National Championship Game became its own game.

Auburn defensive tackle Nick Fairley celebrates after winning the BCS National Championship Game over Oregon on January 10, 2011.

Some fans liked the BCS system. They said the lack of a playoff ensured that every regular-season game was important. But many others were tired of the BCS selecting the final matchup. They wanted to see the best teams settle the championship through a tournament, just as it's done in other sports—and in every other level of college football.

Ultimately, the momentum was too much to ignore. The true championship was conceived on June 26, 2012. A committee of university presidents approved a four-team tournament plan. It was called, simply, the College Football Playoff.

"I think it's tremendous progress," Washington State coach Mike Leach said. He added: "I think it's going to be ridiculously exciting, and it's going to generate a bunch of money."

BCS executive director Bill Hancock was beaming at a news conference following the meetings.

"It's a great day for college football," he said. "As soon as the commissioners realized they could do this and protect the regular season, the light went on for everybody."

Finally, in the 2014 season, the College Football Playoff began.

The system still uses a human element. The College Football Playoff rankings determine the top four teams. A selection committee considers conference championships, strength of schedule, head-to-head results, and comparison of results against common opponents. And in year one, the committee picked Ohio State versus Alabama, and Oregon versus Florida State.

Already this choice of teams showed a major change. In years past, a single loss often eliminated a team from the national title discussion. This year, however, the playoff allowed the Buckeyes to overcome a surprising loss at home to Virginia Tech in September.

The team overcame other setbacks, too. Ohio State's top two quarterbacks had been lost to injuries. Braxton Miller went down before the season started, and then J. T. Barrett was injured in the last regular-season game. That thrust the inexperienced sophomore Jones onto the big stage. He hardly blinked. Jones led the Buckeyes to a win in the Big Ten title game. Then they beat mighty Alabama 42–35 in the Sugar Bowl in the national semifinal. That sent Ohio State to AT&T Stadium in Texas for the first championship game.

Joining the Buckeyes were the Oregon Ducks. They had barreled through the Seminoles 59–20 in the other semifinal, the Rose Bowl. Ohio State would have to slow Oregon's high-octane offense to have a chance. And that's just what happened.

Despite his inexperience, Jones ruled the day. He finished with 242 yards passing and a touchdown. Ohio State racked up 538 yards of total offense. That was enough to easily beat Oregon 42–20.

For many football fans, the playoff was a long-overdue addition to college football. For others, it still didn't go far enough. They wanted eight or even 16 teams. So far, officials have been hesitant, citing the challenges of adding to an already busy schedule for the student athletes. Plus, in its early years, the four-team playoff has worked pretty well.

Sure, there's still going to be disagreement about which teams are selected over those finishing fifth, sixth, seventh, and eighth. The chance of an undefeated team from outside the five most powerful conferences being denied a spot still exists, as Central Florida showed while finishing 13–0 in the 2017 season. Some of the tradition sewn into the rich fabric of the sport had to be sacrificed for the new system. The final game is now played more than a week after the old season-ending marker on New Year's Day.

But the controversy each year is not nearly what it used to be. It's harder for the fifth-best team to gain

> Ohio State fans didn't have to share the national title with any fan base after the 2014 season.

widespread support for a perceived slight than the squad that wound up No. 2 or No. 3 in the past. There's finally an opportunity for the undisputed champion to be determined on the field, rather than in a meeting room or by a committee of voters.

CHAPTER 2

A FATEFUL MEETING

One December day, leaders of the country's most prominent college football programs gathered for a discussion about how to make the game safer. Across the nation, people were increasingly worried about the danger of the sport. This was no ordinary campus meeting, either.

They were at the White House.

The president of the United States was concerned enough about the matter that he summoned coaches and advisers from Harvard and Yale. Their goal was to change the rules of the game.

A drawing depicts an 1879 college football game between Yale and Princeton.

Were it not for that 1905 summit organized by President Theodore Roosevelt, who knows what college football would look like now—or whether it would exist at all.

The first American football game was played on November 6, 1869. Teams from the universities now known as Princeton and Rutgers met in a cow pasture in New Brunswick, New Jersey. There were 25—yes, 25!—players on each side. Perhaps even crazier was the fact that carrying the ball and throwing the ball were both against the rules. The ball could only be moved up and down the field by kicking it or batting it with heads or hands. There were no touchdowns, either. Teams were awarded just one point for each successful kick through the goal posts. Using those rules, Rutgers won 6–4.

The game's popularity grew steadily from there, but so did its viciousness. As a contact sport with players colliding during every snap, football has always had an element of danger. A serious injury can occur at any given moment. With helmets, pads, and a completely different style of play, though, the sport is nothing compared with what it used to be.

In that fateful year of 1905, a total of 18 people reportedly died from injuries they suffered while playing football. Several schools suspended their programs. The president of Harvard, Charles Eliot, was one of the leaders pushing to ban the game altogether.

Roosevelt was a hard-nosed military man who long held an affinity for sports. He was upset, however, by these avoidable deaths of young men. He recognized a problem with the level of violence that was taking place on the field. His own son, who was playing for Harvard's freshman team at the time, was cut badly over the eye during one game.

"Brutality playing a game should awaken the heartiest and most plainly shown contempt for the player guilty of it, especially if this brutality is coupled with a low cunning in committing it without getting caught by the umpire," Roosevelt said

> ❝ Brutality playing a game should awaken the heartiest and most plainly shown contempt for the player guilty of it, especially if this brutality is coupled with a low cunning in committing it without getting caught by the umpire."
> —President Theodore Roosevelt

in his remarks about college football in a gathering of Harvard graduates.

So the Commander in Chief served as a critical negotiator. On one side were the people who wanted football outlawed. On the other side were those who preferred to keep the sport the way it was. A committee assembled to change the rules. The organization now known as the National Collegiate Athletic Association (NCAA) formed during this process.

Two significant twists emerged for the game in this landmark year. First, the forward pass became legal. This change helped spread the players out on the field and kept large groups of players from constantly running into one another in the hunt for the ball. Second, each play was to be stopped when a player fell on the ball. Those pileups were ripe for serious injuries. Instead, teams could regroup, and the offense snapped the ball to restart play.

Passing plays took a while to catch on. Coaches considered passes to be too risky, preferring to run the ball instead. At some programs, that conservative strategy lived on for decades.

Not at Notre Dame. The Fighting Irish were the first team to fully display the power of the pass.

Few teams can challenge Notre Dame when it comes to tradition. Even today, student volunteers paint the team's iconic helmets gold each week. Unlike other schools, Notre Dame still uses simple slash marks, rather than colorful logos, in its end zone. The university has also fiercely maintained independent status in football. With a strong brand all its own, Notre Dame never felt the need to be part of a conference.

These traditions might seem old-fashioned in today's game. But the small Catholic school in small-town Indiana sure showed a progressive spirit on November 1, 1913. Using an aerial attack, the Irish took down a dominant Army team in a 35–13 victory. The Fighting Irish staked out their place on the sport's growing landscape, with quarterback Gus Dorais completing 14 of 17 passes for 243 yards and two touchdowns. One was a 40-yard reception by Knute Rockne. He would become Notre Dame's head coach five years later and go on to be one of its most successful leaders.

"The press and the public and the football public hailed this new game," Rockne said, "and Notre Dame received credit as the originator of a style of play that we simply systematized."

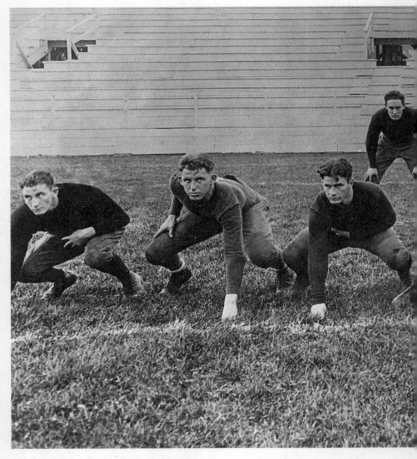

> Notre Dame's 1924 offense poses for a picture, with the iconic "Four Horsemen" in the back.

Many more changes awaited the sport over the next hundred years. So what was next big thing? Helmets. In 1939, the NCAA required that all players

22

wear them. From there, the game began to evolve into the faster-paced, better-protected, higher-profile spectacle that it is today.

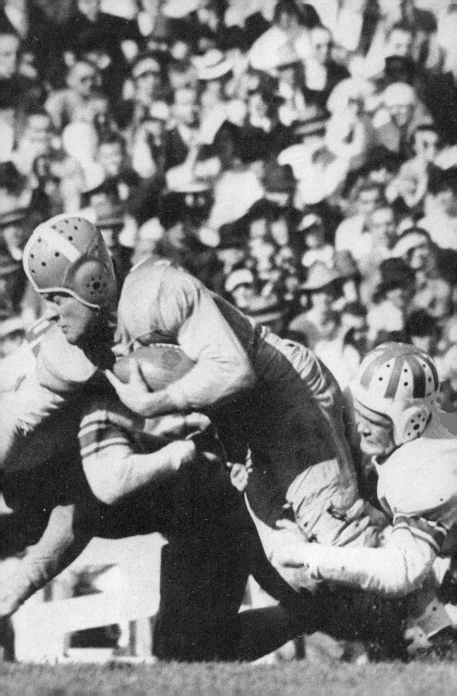

CHAPTER 3

GOING BOWLING

Earnie Seiler was the lead promoter of the Orange Bowl in Miami. The annual game was only a few years old in 1938, but Seiler was determined to grab a bigger share of college football's spotlight. So he traveled all the way to Oklahoma to persuade one of the country's strongest teams to participate.

The day of his visit was unseasonably cold, but the weather worked right into his hands. He brought a bunch of the most beautiful photos of Miami he could find. Using pictures of the palm trees, blue ocean, and white sand, Seiler tried to sell the Sooners on making the long trip east. He had company. Representatives from the Sugar Bowl in New Orleans were on campus, too. So were reps from the Cotton Bowl in Dallas, and they were offering Oklahoma $50,000 to play there.

Oklahoma defenders tackle Tennessee's Leonard Coffman at the Orange Bowl after the 1938 season.

25

Seiler's best guarantee was $25,000. He even paid some fraternity members $10 to write "On to Miami" in chalk on the sidewalks to help build support. In the end, the lure of the beach was too strong to ignore.

"When I came in, the Sugar and Cotton people didn't even give me a second look. They weren't worried a bit. Then I brought out my pictures," Seiler once said in an interview with *Sports Illustrated*. "I said, 'Come to Miami. We'll have ourselves a party.'"

That they did, at least off the field.

The Sooners signed up to play Tennessee, another unbeaten team that season. The game took place on January 2, 1939. It sold out, with more than 32,000 fans packing into a stadium that was supposed to hold only 22,000. They saw an exceptionally physical game that led to several injuries and ejections on both sides. Tennessee grinded out a 17–0 victory. Oklahoma headed home humbled, with one blemish on an otherwise stellar season.

That same day, on the other side of the country, nearly 90,000 fans turned up to watch the Rose Bowl game in Pasadena, California. The Rose Bowl was the premier attraction, the game that Seiler hoped the Orange Bowl could one day replicate. Known as

"The Granddaddy of Them All," the Rose Bowl was the first bowl game, debuting in 1902. The game itself has been played every year since 1916. In addition to that prestige, the game is held at the iconic Rose Bowl stadium, which once seated more than 100,000 people. With the backdrop of the San Gabriel Mountains, the reds and oranges of the late-afternoon California sky, and the breezes off the Pacific Ocean, the Rose Bowl is one of the most famous stadiums in sports.

That Rose Bowl game in 1939 was one of the most memorable, too.

USC, playing only 15 miles from its campus in Los Angeles, was playing Duke, a team from North Carolina that had not allowed a single point all season. Trailing 3–0 late in the fourth quarter, the Trojans turned to fourth-string quarterback Doyle Nave.

There was some miscommunication among the coaching staff that led to Nave going into the game. Nonetheless, Nave completed four consecutive passes to "Antelope" Al Krueger. The last one was a 19-yard touchdown in the closing seconds. USC won the game 7–3.

That was the extent of Nave's football career. He went into the Navy instead.

> **USC players chase down Duke's Dan Hill after an interception at the Rose Bowl on January 2, 1939.**

During World War II (1939–1945), while stationed on an aircraft carrier, Nave met a fellow officer named Dan Hill who had played for Duke in that epic Rose Bowl game.

"I asked Dan whether he had any idea that I was going to pass when I came into the game," Nave said.

The answer was a resounding *no*.

"We didn't even know who you were," Hill told Nave.

With the Rose Bowl well established, other bowl games followed. The Cotton, Sugar, and Orange bowls made up the core four games each New Year's Day. With no national tournament or official championship, this was the way the sport wrapped up each season. The Fiesta Bowl in Arizona became another major event by the 1980s.

For years, bowl games were the highlight of the season. Fans thought of them as mini-championships, often with nationally televised parades to go with the games. Meanwhile, thousands of alumni and students took winter vacations to see their favorite school play football.

Bowl games soon established relationships with conferences. That ensured bowl organizers didn't have to fight over teams as they had in 1939. The Rose Bowl has a long-standing tradition of pitting the Pac-12 and Big Ten conferences against each other. The Southwest Conference once sent its top team to the Cotton Bowl. When that conference dissolved in 1996, half of its teams joined the new Big 12. The Big 12 began sending its champion to the Orange Bowl.

The winner of the Southeastern Conference (SEC), meanwhile, went to the Sugar Bowl.

As the sport grew into a bigger and bigger business, the bowls paid the schools and their conferences even more money to play at their games. For the biggest bowls, payouts were in the millions of dollars.

As the pressure to stage a true title game increased, the traditional tie-ins to the major bowls began to loosen. The Bowl Coalition came first in 1992. Its goal was to get the top two teams to meet in one of the New Year's Day games. Then came the Bowl Alliance. However, both failed to catch on because some bowls held out. The organizers of those games were happy—and well compensated—with the current system. Finally, in the 1998 season, the Rose Bowl signed on to join the new BCS. The BCS ensured the nation's top two teams would play each other, even if there was disagreement about which two teams those were.

The BCS began staging its own game after the 2006 season. This shift allowed the traditional bowls to more frequently select teams from their traditional conferences. Eventually, in 2014, the BCS gave way to the College Football Playoff system that's in place today. The six biggest bowl games take turns hosting a

Stanford players celebrate their win at the 2016 Sun Bowl, one of the oldest midsize bowl games.

semifinal. The winners move on to a stand-alone national title game.

The biggest bowl games remain a fixture at the end of every season. Through the decades, they've also gained a lot of company.

By the 1950s, a handful of smaller bowl games had popped up. There was the Sun Bowl in El Paso, Texas. There was the Gator Bowl in Jacksonville,

Florida. The Tangerine Bowl (now known as the Citrus Bowl) was another big one, taking place in Orlando, Florida. By the 1970s, the regulars included the Peach Bowl in Atlanta, Georgia, the Holiday Bowl in San Diego, California, and the Liberty Bowl in Memphis, Tennessee.

Then the industry really took off in the 21st century. For the 1992 season, there were 18 bowl games. That meant approximately 34 percent of the teams at the NCAA's top level went to a postseason game. Companies and TV networks had figured out that bowl games could be a good way to get exposure or make money. And bowl organizers were happy to oblige. So by the 2017 season, the number of bowl games had risen to 40. That meant 80 of the 130 teams playing at the top level played in a postseason game. The lineup wasn't as prestigious as it once was, with games such as the Bad Boy Mowers Gasparilla Bowl in St. Petersburg, Florida, the Famous Idaho Potato Bowl in Boise, Idaho, and the Bahamas Bowl in, yes, the Bahamas. But the allure of a holiday trip to a tropical site remained a popular part of the sport.

Winning a major bowl like the Orange Bowl is still a thrill for players like Florida State's Dalvin Cook, who won in December 2016.

CHAPTER 4

INCREDIBLE ENDINGS

Notre Dame and Michigan State were tied 10–10 on a chilly November afternoon in East Lansing, Michigan. The top two teams in the 1966 polls were both undefeated, duking it out on the field to essentially decide the national championship. There were larger issues at stake, too. Michigan State was attracting extra attention as one of the first major universities to fully integrate black players on its team.

The lead-up to the game created a ton of interest. An NCAA rule allowed only one national TV appearance per team each season. As such, the ABC network was planning to show the game only in the north. More

 A huge crowd fills the stadium to watch Michigan State host Notre Dame in 1966.

than 50,000 fans wrote letters to the network trying to have the game shown across the country instead. Thousands of others signed petitions. The campaign worked. In fact, the game was even shown to US troops overseas in Vietnam, the first time that had happened.

All of those viewers were treated to a tight game. Late in the fourth quarter, the score remained tied 10–10. With a little more than a minute left in the game, the Spartans punted. The Fighting Irish took the ball back at their own 30-yard line. They had plenty of time to go for a touchdown. And if that failed, they could at least move into position for the winning field goal. But that's not what Notre Dame coach Ara Parseghian opted to do.

The Fighting Irish didn't throw a pass on any of their last six plays. Their final snap was a quarterback sneak, guaranteeing that the game would end in, gulp, a tie.

"We think we are the best," Michigan State coach Duffy Daugherty said. "I don't think anyone can say Notre Dame is better than us. We both deserve the national championship."

The controversies over national championships prior to the College Football Playoff weren't the only instances when this sport couldn't produce a winner. Overtime wasn't included at the NCAA's top level until 1996. If two teams were tied at the end of the fourth quarter, that was the way the game ended.

So why did Notre Dame play it so safe that day?

The Fighting Irish were missing their starting quarterback, running back, and center by that point in the game. They had also missed a 41-yard field goal the last time they had the ball. Meanwhile, Michigan State had a strong kicker. Parseghian didn't want to risk a turnover that would give the Spartans the ball deep in Notre Dame's territory.

The national championship was part of his thinking, too. This was Michigan State's last game of the season. The team won its second straight Big Ten title, which typically mean a berth to the Rose Bowl. But the Rose Bowl didn't allow teams to play there in consecutive years, and the Big Ten allowed only one team each year to go to a bowl game. So the Spartans were out of luck. They would have no more opportunities to pass Notre Dame in the polls.

Alabama was also a strong team that year, but the final rankings at the time were revealed prior to the bowl games. Notre Dame had one game left against

USC. The Fighting Irish won 51–0, assuring their place on top.

"If I was sure a tie would make me No. 1 in the polls, I would rather be ranked No. 1. Five, 10, 15 years from now, that's what people will remember, that you were the top team in the country," Parseghian said.

He took plenty of criticism for his strategy, and the Spartans were upset that day by the way the game ended. In time, though, they realized the position Notre Dame was in.

"Putting the ball in the air would have been foolish on his part," Michigan State linebacker Charlie Thornhill said 30 years later.

Bowl games usually bring celebration, but not always stiff competition. With long layoffs after the end of the regular season, teams sometimes lose focus. There have been plenty of blowouts in those December and New Year's Day games. But sometimes those bowl games turn out to be the best contests imaginable. That was the case on January 2, 1984, when Nebraska met Miami in the Orange Bowl.

The Huskers were ranked first in the AP poll during the entire 1983 season. They dominated almost every team they played. Nebraska scored 84 points in one

Spartans coach Duffy Daugherty (left) and Irish coach Ara Parseghian share the 1966 MacArthur Bowl, awarded to the national champion.

game, a nonconference victory at Minnesota. The Huskers met their match in fifth-ranked Miami, though, against a Hurricanes team conveniently playing on its home field.

39

> Miami's Tolbert Bain (left) and Melvin Bratton celebrate their win over Nebraska in the Orange Bowl.

Miami built a 17–0 lead and was still ahead 31–17 in the fourth quarter. Until Nebraska charged back. The Huskers scored a touchdown with 48 seconds left to cut the lead to 31–30. Earlier in the day, second-ranked Texas had lost in the Cotton Bowl to Georgia. That left Nebraska as the only unbeaten team in the country.

So a tie with Miami almost certainly would have given the Huskers the consensus national championship.

But coach Tom Osborne strayed from his normally conservative approach. Instead of settling for the extra point and the probable tie, Osborne called for a two-point conversion attempt. Unlike Parseghian at Notre Dame some 17 years earlier, he wanted to go for the win. This time, it didn't pay off. Turner Gill passed into the end zone but Miami's Ken Calhoun knocked it down, preserving the victory for the Hurricanes. The writers and the coaches were so impressed by the performance that Miami was voted No. 1 in the final polls, leapfrogging a handful of teams.

> ❝ I thought if you were going to win a national championship, you had to win."
>
> —Nebraska coach Tom Osborne

"I thought if you were going to win a national championship, you had to win," Osborne said in defense of his decision.

Miami had some setbacks the following season, none more memorable than on November 23, 1984. The Hurricanes hosted Boston College on a rainy, windy afternoon the day after Thanksgiving. The Eagles were enjoying a special season behind quarterback Doug Flutie. Standing just 5-foot-9, Flutie went on to set the all-time NCAA record for career passing yards that year. He won the Heisman Trophy, too. But he is most remembered for one long throw that November day at the Orange Bowl stadium.

Miami led 45–41 in an already wild back-and-forth game. Boston College had time for one last play near midfield with six seconds left. Flutie took the snap, scrambled to avoid a sack, and rolled to his right. He let it fly from his own 37-yard line, and the ball soared into the end zone. Somehow, it slipped through a pack of orange Hurricanes jerseys and found the hands of Eagles wide receiver Gerard Phelan for a touchdown to win the game.

"I think Americans love to root for the underdog, and certainly Boston College and Doug Flutie were underdogs," Phelan said years later. "Here was a scrambling, get-it-done-any-way-you-can kind of guy who had good grades and didn't get into trouble. Everybody was rooting for that guy to win."

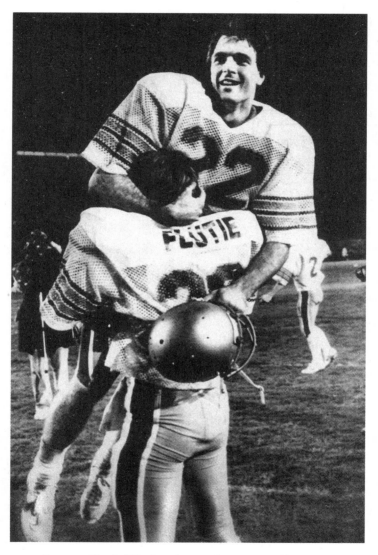

Darren Flutie lifts brother and Boston College teammate Doug Flutie after their miraculous comeback against Miami in 1984.

CHAPTER 5

THE FIERCEST FOES

Before John Elway became known for his clutch performances with the Denver Broncos, and before he was the first overall pick in the draft, he was a senior quarterback for Stanford trying to finish the 1982 season with a win on the road against rival California.

Elway had just moved the Cardinal in position for a 35-yard field goal. With four seconds left, they made it, giving them a 20–19 lead. Game over, right? All that was left was the kickoff. The Bears' only hope was an improbable touchdown return.

Before the kick, Stanford took a 15-yard penalty for excessive celebration. The Cardinal players had

Stanford band members mistakenly rushed the field thinking their team had beaten rival Cal in 1982.

swarmed the field in the excitement of the dramatic and certain victory. This all prompted Stanford to try a short kickoff, called a squib, that is typically harder to catch and return.

Kevin Moen fielded the ball for the Bears at his own 43-yard line. Just before being tackled, he lateraled it back to teammate Richard Rodgers near the sideline. Rodgers tossed the ball to Dwight Garner, who flipped it back to Rodgers right before three Stanford players brought him down. Rodgers then tossed it to Mariet Ford as he stumbled around midfield, but advancement still appeared unlikely.

That's what Stanford's band members believed anyway. The musical men and women began to file onto the field from the back of the end zone, eager to revel in the win.

Ford made it to the 25-yard line, but several Stanford tacklers trapped him. Then Moen came back into the picture, seemingly out of nowhere, to snag a here-goes-nothing, over-the-shoulder lateral from Ford. And all of a sudden, the red-clad band members had mixed in with the players on the field, causing mass confusion. Moen had a full head of steam and zipped right through, amazingly making it to the end zone.

"The band is out on the field!" Cal radio announcer Joe Starkey cried. "The most amazing, sensational, dramatic, heart-rending, exciting, thrilling finish in the history of college football!"

Moen conked a trombone player on the head with the ball, as the celebration quickly shifted from Stanford's stunned fans to Cal's. In the rivalry known as "The Big Game," the strung-together kickoff return by the Bears became known as "The Play."

"Why did it work?" Moen said years later. "Because we never practiced it. We just did it. It just so happened the pieces fit together."

Stanford, to no avail, argued that Garner's knee touched the ground before his toss to Rodgers. There was no replay review then and no way to determine that after the fact.

"This was an insult to college football. There's no way it should have happened," Elway said in the heat of the frustration after the game, criticizing the officials. "They ruined my last college football game. It's unbelievable."

Stanford and California first played football against each other in 1892. These prestigious Pac-12 universities in Palo Alto and Berkeley, respectively, sit approximately 50 miles apart on opposite ends of San Francisco Bay. They play for the Stanford Axe, a wooden plaque with a red axe blade affixed to the front. The scores of all of the games between the two teams are listed beneath it.

In the Big Ten, Minnesota and Wisconsin play for an actual axe. It's Paul Bunyan's Axe, to be precise, in honor of the fictional giant lumberjack. In the famous folk tales, Bunyan was credited with creating part of the landscape of the northern United States. The wooden handle is six feet long, bearing the results of the all-time series. The Gophers and Badgers used to award the winner the "Slab of Bacon" trophy until it went missing in the 1940s.

Regardless of the prize, though, these two teams from bordering states have played longer than any other foes in major college football history. The first Minnesota–Wisconsin game was in 1890. The winning team used to parade the axe around the stadium and pretend to chop down one of the goalposts, a celebration that didn't always sit well if the home team lost. In 2013 at Minnesota's stadium, some of the Gophers players stood in their end zone to protect their goalpost. The Badgers were taken aback by the

Wisconsin players celebrate after winning Paul Bunyan's Axe in 2016.

sudden change in protocol. Shoving and shouting ensued. The following year, the axe was awarded to the winning team in the locker room to avoid any more incidents, though winners still celebrated on the field.

Those are the kind of hard feelings that exist between many rivals around the country. Most of these storied contests take place between schools either in the same state or in bordering states. Often, families and communities are divided between their rooting interest, depending on where they went to college or which team they better identify with. Sometimes the culture around the university plays into the rivalry. It could feature a public school versus a private school. Or a game might pit a prestigious state university known for medical research against a public school rooted in agriculture or education. Many times, they're competing for the same conference championships. And when players get only four or five tries to experience a win over a rival, the intensity only increases.

Michigan and Ohio State have historically dominated the Big Ten. So it's no surprise they boast the conference's premier rivalry.

"As a kid growing up, Ohio State–Michigan was Christmas Day, the biggest day of the year," former Buckeyes quarterback and current ESPN analyst Kirk Herbstreit once wrote.

One thing not on the line when they play, however, is a clever trophy. Minnesota plays for more than just the axe. The Gophers and Iowa Hawkeyes play for the Floyd of Rosedale trophy. That's a 98-pound bronze pig, a prize instituted in 1935 and inspired by the farming tradition in both states. Perhaps the most famous trophy goes to the winner of Michigan and

The annual Michigan–Ohio State game is often a battle between two of the nation's top teams.

Minnesota. They have been playing since 1892. In those early years, both teams were among the best in the sport. So when the Wolverines traveled to Minneapolis in 1903, coach Fielding Yost didn't want to take any chances. He got a big jug to hold water for his team, ensuring they had clean water to drink. When the game ended in a tie, Yost and his team were in such a hurry to get out that they forgot the jug. Minnesota kept it as a trophy.

The teams didn't play again for six years. But when they did, Minnesota's athletic director offered to return the jug—if the Wolverines could win it back. This time, Michigan went home with their water jug, and the two teams have been playing for the Little Brown Jug ever since.

Michigan and Michigan State play for the Paul Bunyan trophy, a statue of the mythical man. Indiana and Purdue square off for the Old Oaken Bucket. There's a gold chain attached to it, with a bunch of I's and P's to mark which team won each year.

Not all great rivalries need a trophy. Out west, Oregon and Oregon State meet in the "Civil War." Washington and Washington State play for the Apple Cup, a nod to the state's top produce. UCLA and USC fight for the Victory Bell, which originated from a railroad engine. To the south, Oklahoma and Texas vie for the Golden Hat. Mississippi and Mississippi State meet for the Golden Egg.

Then there's the Iron Bowl, the annual battle between SEC heavyweights Alabama and Auburn in one of the most football-fanatical states in the country. After Alabama won the national championship in 2009, Auburn took the next title. Then Alabama won the following two. In 2013 their annual late-November matchup was tied 28–28 when Alabama coach Nick Saban sent his kicker out to try a last-second 57-yard

Auburn's Chris Davis runs back his "Kick Six" touchdown against Alabama in 2013.

field goal. The ball was on line but fell a bit short, where Auburn's Chris Davis was waiting to catch it.

Teams are allowed to run back failed field goals, and that's just what Davis did. He raced up the left sideline and cut back to the middle of the field to complete his 109-yard sprint and give the Tigers a 34–28 victory.

Auburn went on to the BCS National Championship Game, only to lose to Florida State. But the Tigers and their fans had an experience to savor as strong as any title. The "Kick Six" is how that play is often referred to now.

CHAPTER 6

CLASSIC COACHES

It was January 8, 2018. Through two quarters of the College Football Playoff title game, the Georgia Bulldogs looked like the better team. Taking advantage of playing in their home state, they built up a 13–0 lead over Nick Saban and the Alabama Crimson Tide. Against Saban, though, no lead is safe.

Alabama quarterback Jalen Hurts was struggling. So Saban made the bold move to bring in freshman Tua Tagovailoa for the second half. The gutsy move paid off. Though his experience was limited, Tagovailoa looked the part of a seasoned leader. Before long, the Tide was right back in the game. And after 60 minutes, the teams were tied 20–20.

Georgia began the extra session with a field goal. Alabama would have to at least match in order to stay

Nick Saban set a new standard for coaching success with Alabama.

alive. Tagovailoa made that a lot harder on the Tide's first offensive play. He was sacked for a 16-yard loss. But on the next snap, the left-handed native of Hawaii dropped back in the pocket. He zipped a perfect pass up the sideline to a streaking DeVonta Smith. With the 41-yard touchdown, Alabama had its fifth national title in just 11 years under Saban. One year after a heartbreaking, last-second loss to Clemson in the national title game, Alabama was back on the winning side.

"I could not believe it," Saban said after the game. "There's lots of highs and lows. Last year we lost on the last play of the game, and this year we won on the last play of the game. These kids really responded the right way. We said last year, 'Don't waste the feeling.' They sure didn't."

Including one at LSU, Saban's six major poll championships matched the total of Paul "Bear" Bryant, who launched the last Alabama dynasty in the 1960s.

The game has seen many legendary coaches over the years. Bobby Bowden at Florida State. Joe Paterno at Penn State. Tom Osborne at Nebraska. Woody Hayes at Ohio State, where Urban Meyer went after taking

Bear Bryant led Alabama to 25 winning seasons and six national titles, beginning in 1958.

Florida to two titles. But Saban has managed to remain at the head of the pack.

With 11 all-time finishes on top of the AP poll, Alabama has never been a place to settle for less than excellence. Saban's time there has only taken that determination for winning higher. Some of the best college football coaches are often some of the strictest and demanding people. Playing for a no-nonsense coach like Saban is not for everyone. A team-first, hardworking attitude is important at any school, but nowhere is it more ingrained in the culture than with Saban's Crimson Tide. He speaks often of "the process," an attention to detail and a commitment to preparation that must come long before Saturday kickoffs. Alabama has the winning tradition and the state-of-the-art facilities to attract the best recruits in the country. But the Crimson Tide couldn't be this successful without doing the work.

The seeds of success for Saban were sown in the mountains of West Virginia, where he was raised. Most people in his hometown worked in the coal mines, but his father, Nick Saban Sr., ran a service station and a Dairy Queen ice-cream shop so he could avoid that dangerous work. He wanted to keep his son out of it, too. One day, after Saban received a D in eighth grade music for refusing to sing in front of the class, his father took him down the mineshaft for a tour.

"If you don't get an education, this is where you're going to end up," Saban recounted. "So that was the last time I ever went down there. I have a tremendous amount of respect for all the people who are coal miners, but it's not something I wanted to do."

> " My dad was the hardest-working man I've ever seen. He was demanding, and that could be hard. But he set the bar for me at a very young age, a work ethic that has never gone away."
> —Alabama coach
> Nick Saban

Saban was the quarterback for Monongah High School, helping the Lions win the state championship in 1968.

"My dad was the hardest-working man I've ever seen," he said. "He was demanding, and that could be hard. But he set the bar for me at a very young age, a work ethic that has never gone away."

Like every successful leader, the best coaches didn't become who they were without the support of

Darrell Royal and his coaching staff at Texas
revolutionized the sport with his Wishbone offense.

their staffs. Darrell Royal won a national championship with Texas in 1963, but the Longhorns were in a slump a few years later as pressure from the rabid fans rose. Royal needed a spark for his proud program, so he turned the offense over to an assistant coach named Emory Bellard. Bellard produced a system that became known as the Wishbone, a triple-option scheme that lined up a fullback and two halfbacks behind the quarterback to make a "Y" shape.

The quarterback could either fake a handoff to the fullback or quickly give him the ball, depending on which way the defensive tackle was going. Then if he kept the ball, the quarterback could either run it himself or pitch it to one of his halfbacks to try to run wide around the defense. Many other teams copied it during the era, some putting their own twist on it, but Texas under Royal and Bellard was the inventor. The innovation was well timed. The Longhorns went on to win national championships in 1969 and 1970. They had a 30-game winning streak at one point.

The Wishbone worked because it confused opponents. But it was also a simple, safe style to run. Royal once said, "Three things can happen when you pass, and two of them are bad."

The legend of Glenn "Pop" Warner (right) lives on through the youth leagues named after him.

The earlier eras produced plenty of pioneers of the sport, too. Walter Camp was the coach at Yale who was credited with creating the line of scrimmage, where the blockers must start before each play to lessen the load of the collisions. Camp, who was on every rules commission the sport had through 1925, also invented the center snap as a way of beginning each play.

And don't forget Glenn "Pop" Warner. He thought of the huddle, the three-point stance for offensive linemen, pads for shoulders and thighs, numbers on player jerseys, and so much more over a coaching career that took him to Pittsburgh, Stanford, and Temple. He helped steer college football into the new era, after President Theodore Roosevelt helped usher in rule changes to make the game safer. Pop Warner youth leagues continue to this day across the country, designed to teach kids a safe way to play.

CHAPTER 7

THE HEISMAN POSE

Desmond Howard backpedaled to catch the punt at Michigan's 7-yard line. He planted his foot. Then he burst forward to wiggle away from an Ohio State defender. Howard was on his way.

He slipped past two more tacklers before the 25. With another acceleration, Howard veered left toward the sideline with only one more man to beat. Naturally, Howard won that footrace. He coasted down the field with nobody in reach. As he crossed the goal line, ABC announcer Keith Jackson crooned, "Hello Heisman!" Then Howard struck the pose, lifting his left leg and extending his left arm with the ball tucked into his

 Desmond Howard was a standout wide receiver and return specialist for the Michigan Wolverines.

> **The iconic Heisman Trophy is named for John Heisman, a former player who became an innovative head coach.**

right side. He was mimicking the Heisman Trophy, the bronze sculpture of a stiff-arming ball-carrier given to the best player in the country every year since 1935.

Howard had good reason for the bold display on behalf of the Big Ten champion Wolverines. The Ohio State game was Michigan's last of the 1991 regular season, and by then Howard was well on his way to winning the Heisman. In doing so, he'd become just the third wide receiver to win the award. Nebraska's Johnny Rodgers in 1972 and Notre Dame's Tim Brown in 1987 were the only others.

Howard caught 62 passes for 985 yards and 19 touchdowns that year. Plus, he added two more rushing scores and one each as a punt returner and a kickoff returner. His nickname, fittingly, was "Magic." Howard was the first wide receiver to lead the Big Ten in scoring that year, and he set or tied five NCAA records.

Michigan was ranked in the top seven of the AP poll all season. It was one of the finest seasons in the history of the hallowed program. Howard helped set the tone in a September game against rival Notre Dame. He leaped forward with fully outstretched arms to catch a fourth-down pass from Elvis Grbac and landed in the end zone in control of the ball. That feat, forever known by Michigan fans as "The Catch," helped seal the victory that afternoon. It also set in motion Howard's campaign for college football's ultimate individual award.

"There's no doubt that catch made me a candidate for the Heisman," Howard said. "I didn't think much about anything but catching the ball at the time it happened, but when I went home that night and watched it on TV, I could see how spectacular it was."

Howard won by the fourth-largest voting margin in the history of the award, easily beating the second-place finisher, Florida State quarterback Casey Weldon.

Howard, who's now an analyst for ESPN, went on to an 11-year career in the National Football League (NFL). Though he didn't make much of an impact as a wide receiver, his return skills grew even stronger. Playing for the Green Bay Packers, Howard helped the team reach the Super Bowl after the 1996 season. After taking a kickoff back for a score in the Super Bowl—his fifth TD return of the season—he was named the game's Most Valuable Player. He's still the only special teams player to win the award.

Not all of the Heisman Trophy winners enjoy such post-college success. Running back Archie Griffin, the only two-time winner of the award, totaled only 13 touchdowns in seven NFL seasons. Quarterbacks like Gino Torretta (1992), Jason White (2003), and Johnny Manziel (2012), for one reason or another, never panned out in the NFL.

Sometimes, the circumstance is tragic.

Ernie Davis was a great running back for Syracuse, where he broke fellow Orangeman Jim Brown's career records. Davis also was part of the Orangemen's only national championship, which they won in 1959. And in 1961, Davis became the first black player to win the Heisman Trophy. Yet for all of his success, Davis was perhaps admired even more for his gentlemanly demeanor. He helped break down racial barriers in the sport. The day Davis accepted the Heisman Trophy at the ceremony in New York, President John F. Kennedy happened to be visiting. The president even asked to meet Davis, not the other way around.

"Ernie made it beautiful for that new era of championship guys," Brown said in an interview with *Sports Illustrated*. "Dynamite dudes, black guys, came to Syracuse after Ernie. Floyd Little and Jim Nance and others. It was fantastic. They could go there without losing their dignity. I was fighting every day at Syracuse to hold on to my dignity. I broke through, but Ernie created the new era."

The Washington Redskins made Davis the first pick in the 1962 NFL Draft and then traded him to the Cleveland Browns. Their plan was to pair him with Brown and form a dominant backfield. But Davis was stricken with the most severe form of leukemia, a cancer of the blood. He died in 1963.

Syracuse's Ernie Davis was a dominant running back on the 1959 national championship team.

Sometimes, elite players like Davis have a special charisma that only adds to their legend as one of the game's greats. Florida quarterback Tim Tebow was one of those.

Since the Heisman Trophy was first awarded in 1935, the winners had all been juniors or seniors. In 2007, Tebow made history by becoming the first sophomore winner. Since Tebow, more sophomores have won. Even freshmen Manziel of Texas A&M (2012) and Jameis Winston of Florida State (2013) have claimed the sport's top individual honor. But few players have had the lasting impact on the game that Tebow had.

Tebow ran the spread offense under coach Urban Meyer, using his strength, toughness, and speed to run the ball as well as he threw it. Many fans also appreciated Tebow's values. Having grown up in a family of Christian missionaries, he took offseason trips to the Philippines to work at an orphanage.

His leadership ability was never more on display than after a surprising defeat by Mississippi early in his junior year. Tebow apologized to Florida fans for not being able to complete an unbeaten season. Then he made what's known in Gators lore as "the promise."

A true dual-threat quarterback, Tim Tebow kept Florida among the best teams in the nation.

Meyer was so impressed he had it put on a plaque the next year.

"You will never see any player in the entire country play as hard as I will the rest of the season. You will never see someone push the rest of the team as hard

as I will push everybody the rest of the season," a glum Tebow said after that game. "You will never see a team play as hard as we will the rest of the season. God bless."

No team came within 10 points of the Gators the rest of their way to the national championship.

CHAPTER 8

SMALL SCHOOLS, BIG TRADITIONS

The town of Grambling, Louisiana, is tucked into the woods of the northern part of the state. It's population is only around 5,000. Grambling State University isn't so remote in the world of college football, though, thanks to Eddie Robinson.

Hired by the historically black school in 1941 to teach and coach football, Robinson spent 57 years trying to mold young men into professionals—whether they continued their football career past college or not. Grambling sent more than 100 players to the NFL under Robinson's watch, despite being in a lower tier of the NCAA's Division I. That list included

Few have come close to the success of Grambling State coach Eddie Robinson, who won 408 games over 56 years.

Doug Williams, who in 1988 became the first black quarterback to play in a Super Bowl.

Working on a tight budget, Robinson did just about everything for the team, especially at the beginning. He mowed the grass and taped players' ankles. He even wrote game stories for the local newspaper. When Grambling had a road game, Robinson would fix sandwiches for his players. Like other black people, they weren't allowed to eat in the restaurants in the South until segregation ended in the 1960s.

In Robinson's second season, in 1942, the Tigers went unbeaten and didn't allow a point all year. Robinson wound up winning 408 games, the third-most by any coach in college football history. There's even a street named after him in Baton Rouge, Louisiana, the site of downstate rival Southern University. Grambling won 17 Southwestern Athletic Conference championships and nine black college titles. However, the Tigers never won a national championship and only occasionally made the playoffs. Humble to his core, Robinson was never compelled to pursue a job at a more prominent place.

"People have said at times, 'Why don't you leave?'" Robinson once said. "Leave for what? You know wherever they're going to bring me, they're going to bring me to coach football. They sure aren't going to have me teach science."

The number of Grambling players who turned pro proved that their talent was often on par with the bigger programs around the country. Decades of prejudice kept the black colleges largely out of the spotlight on Saturdays. But in 1991, the TV network NBC decided to televise Grambling's annual game against Southern for a national audience. The Bayou Classic, played at a neutral site in New Orleans, spotlighted a wealth of celebration and tradition that many Americans were unaware of. That includes the "battle of the bands," one of the liveliest halftime shows around.

"Once we saw what kind of game and spectacle it was, it didn't take much to convince us," NBC vice president Ken Schanzer said during the week of the first broadcast. "Sometimes you don't see every tile in the mosaic of American sports. This is definitely one of those tiles."

The smaller colleges will never make as much money from playing football as schools like Alabama, Michigan, and Texas, but the tradition is no less strong.

Sometimes tradition is based on success. North Dakota State won five NCAA Division II championships from 1983 to 1990. After moving up one level to what's now known as the Football Championship Subdivision (FCS), the Bison won five national titles in a row from 2011 to 2015. Then they added another one in 2017. In Division III, Mount Union, a private liberal arts university in Ohio, won 13 championships since 1993 under coach Larry Kehres and later with his son Vince Kehres. The Purple Raiders were runners-up seven other times through 2017.

Sometimes tradition is based on history. Lafayette and Lehigh, two FCS rivals in Pennsylvania, have played more times than any other pair of teams in college football history. They had their 153rd meeting in 2017.

And sometimes tradition comes from a whole host of sources—success, history, geography, and maybe even a little bit of good fortune. One of the fiercest rivalries in Division III is in Minnesota, between Catholic universities St. John's and St. Thomas. Johnnies coach John Gagliardi retired in 2012 with 489 wins, the most in college football history. The Tommies reached the national championship game in 2012 and 2015, losing to Mount Union.

Quarterback Carson Wentz won national titles every year he played at North Dakota State from 2012 to 2015.

> **The rivalry between St. Thomas (left) and St. John's (right) remains one of the fiercest in Division III.**

The two teams first played football on Thanksgiving Day in 1901. A 16-year-old freshman named Ignatius O'Shaughnessy had a starring role for St. John's. Two months later, he was kicked out of school for skipping a church service to have a party in the woods. So he took the train home, only to get off early and walk to the St. Thomas campus. There, he ran into the school president, a priest who warmed to O'Shaughnessy's

honesty and gave him a hot meal and enrolled him right then and there. O'Shaughnessy became not only a football star for St. Thomas but also its biggest supporter. After graduating, he went into business and made a fortune in the oil industry. He gave millions of dollars to his alma mater, and several buildings on the campus bear his name today.

"A man with money," O'Shaughnessy once said, "has the responsibility of putting it to good use."

CHAPTER 9

THE GAME'S GREATEST RITUALS

Picture this: More than 70,000 people are packed into Husky Stadium on a crisp autumn Saturday afternoon, watching the Washington Huskies play the rival Oregon Ducks. The partial metal roof that hangs over the upper deck on each side, looking like wings, helps make the noise of the crowd even louder. The orange sun begins to set behind the Olympic Mountains. The skyscrapers of downtown Seattle sit just five miles to the south, rising above the tree line. Sailboats anchored in Union Bay dot the blue water, resting just beyond the open end of the stadium.

Fans in Husky Stadium and in boats outside cheer on the Washington Huskies.

"The greatest setting in college football" is what the University of Washington calls it, and it's hard to argue with that opinion.

Built in 1920 and remodeled in 2013, Husky Stadium is one of the 15 largest football facilities on a college campus in the country. Some of the fans actually arrive not by land but by sea. Yes, there's room for 150 boats in Husky Harbor, where pregame refreshments are served up aquatic style by the sailing fans who commute from Lake Washington. There's a shuttle service that takes people straight from their boats to the gate.

"I'd put it out there by itself as the grandest view in all of sports," longtime ABC college football announcer Keith Jackson said. "I've hit most of the major stadiums in the world, and I don't remember one that offers that."

One of the true charms of college football is the lively atmosphere created at so many colleges and universities around the country during game day. Students, parents, alumni, and locals transform the campuses into seas of their school's colors, like the purple Washington fans wear to Husky Stadium. Footballs are thrown, beanbags are tossed, and hamburgers are grilled. The fans turn ordinary parking lots or grass fields into big parties before kickoff and even during the game for folks who don't have tickets.

There's plenty of competition for Washington, of course, when it comes to the best scenes on campus. Kenan Stadium at North Carolina, cozily circled by a grove of pine trees, offers another classic photo op. The same goes for Georgia, where the playing field is surrounded by a row of neatly trimmed hedges.

There's Ohio State, where halftime shows at 104,000-seat Ohio Stadium are a tradition unto themselves. The highlight is when the marching band lines up to spell the word *Ohio*, with one member, or occasionally a celebrity, symbolically dotting the *i* in Ohio. At Michigan Stadium, crowds max out at 107,000, the largest in college football, to watch the maize-and-blue Wolverines in their multistriped helmets. Why such a strange design? They were made to look that way long ago so Michigan quarterbacks so could see their receivers down the field more easily. Students at Wisconsin giddily await the end of the third quarter at Camp Randall Stadium, where they shake the concrete by bobbing up and down in rhythm to the rap song "Jump Around."

Thousands of Ole Miss fans tailgate in "The Grove" before home games.

At Mississippi, fans gather for tailgating at "The Grove," a spot in the center of campus shaded by large oak trees. Rebels fans line the sidewalks to cheer the players as they walk to the stadium for the games. Tiger Stadium at LSU was once dubbed "Death Valley."

When the seats are packed for another electric night game in the SEC, Tiger Stadium is a nightmare for opponents. Clemson's Memorial Stadium is known as "Death Valley," too. Those Tigers play in one of the loudest venues in the game.

The service academies have a long, rich history of college football, as well. The Army–Navy game remains one of the most-watched each season regardless of how strong each team is. The final game of the regular season is primarily played in Philadelphia, and the military men and women from each side stand in full uniform throughout the stadium.

Boise State was a latecomer to major college football. No matter, the Broncos have had one of the best winning percentages in the country since moving to the highest level in 1996. How did they first make a name for themselves? By playing in a stadium with a playing surface made of blue, not green, artificial turf.

Gene Bleymaier was the athletic director who came up with the idea. Bothered by a $750,000 price tag for a routine replacement of the old green turf in 1986, he thought of the idea while on an airplane.

"They know it's not grass, so there's really no reason it needs to be green," Bleymaier once said. "Why not do it in our school colors?"

That was before the Broncos moved up to what's now called the Football Bowl Subdivision (FBS).

"It was our way of creating a home-field advantage," Bleymaier said. "When you've got a Nebraska or

> The annual Army–Navy football game is loaded with pageantry and traditions.

Wisconsin, a lot of places around the country, it's all red, all orange or whatever, and it can be intimidating. So why not have a blue field, which is one of our colors, and try to create a home-field advantage?"

CHAPTER 10

SHIFTING LANDSCAPES AND STRETCHING FOOTPRINTS

For all the tradition baked into college football, there have been several staggering changes to the sport over the 100-plus years since it came to be.

Sit back and think about it for a few seconds. Helmets used to be optional. Teams once played only eight or nine games per season. Television wasn't even invented when the Rose Bowl was already an annual event.

The game's gradually shifting landscape began to be altered much more significantly in the early 1990s. The Southwest Conference had been founded in 1914.

 In a blast from the past, Georgia center Brandon Kublanow poses with an old leather helmet in 2016.

It was one of the oldest and proudest leagues in the sport. But by the 1990s it was slipping. Texas A&M was still strong, but several of the other teams in the Texas-based conference were struggling.

In 1992, Arkansas left for the more-prominent SEC. Two years later, heavyweights Texas and Texas A&M announced with Baylor and Texas Tech that they'd be leaving for a new league. In 1996, they combined with the Big Eight to create the Big 12. That left four Southwest teams with no home. Rice, Southern Methodist, and Texas Christian joined the Western Athletic Conference. Houston went with Conference USA.

"It's like a good friend dying," former Texas Tech coach Spike Dykes said years later. "You hate it, and there's not anything you can do about it, but you darn sure can have great memories."

> It's like a good friend dying. You hate it, and there's not anything you can do about it, but you darn sure can have great memories."
>
> –former Texas Tech coach Spike Dykes

The Southwest Conference's final football season was 1995.

"I was excited about the Big 12, but being someone who had grown up in Texas and coached in the SWC for a long time, it was a sad thing," former Texas A&M coach R. C. Slocum said.

Less than 20 years later, football fans in the Lone Star State were disappointed again. Texas A&M left the Big 12 to join the mighty SEC. That meant an end to the Thanksgiving games against Texas. Missouri, too, was heading for the SEC and leaving behind an intense Big 12 rivalry with Kansas. But they weren't alone in leaving the Big 12. Colorado joined the Pac-10, along with Utah, to create the Pac-12. Meanwhile, Nebraska departed for the Big Ten, ending the Thanksgiving weekend tradition of playing Oklahoma, a game that many times determined the national champion.

The money coming to the schools from television contracts was the driving force. Conferences began starting their own cable networks, with the Big Ten going first in 2007. To increase the value of their product to advertisers, the Big Ten needed more schools. So in addition to Nebraska, they brought in Maryland from the Atlantic Coast Conference (ACC) and Rutgers from the Big East. That expanded the conference's territory to the Baltimore–Washington and New York markets.

By 2014, the ACC, Big Ten, and SEC had all swelled to 14 teams. The Big 12 was down to 10. (Hey, there was no need to change the name if the Big Ten wasn't going to.) The Pac-10, more concerned about accuracy, indeed became the Pac-12. Suddenly, these conferences stretched well beyond their original geographic areas. The Big Ten covered 11 states, from Nebraska to New Jersey. The ACC stretched from Massachusetts to Florida. SEC country reached 11 states, too, on a line from Missouri to South Carolina and every state south of it. The Big 12 became just as awkward, including West Virginia and Texas Christian to go with original Big Eight member Iowa State.

The less-prominent FBS conferences were shaken up, too, as a result. The Big East dropped football, with those programs joining the American Athletic Conference. Conference USA gained 14 teams over a 10-year period from 2005 to 2014 but lost 12 (though not all had football programs). The Western Athletic Conference went away, too. Its successor, the Mountain West Conference, carried on the torch of successful midsize programs such as Air Force, Colorado State, and San Diego State.

The game's popularity hasn't fallen off, even if some of the fondest traditions have ended. So what's next for the sport that has been an autumn fixture in America since before there was electricity? Only time will tell,

Missouri crashed the SEC by reaching the conference title game in 2013 and 2014, its second and third seasons in the league.

though more changes are sure to come as the most powerful programs continue to jockey for revenue and chase national championships. What's almost certain is that, no matter what the game looks like in another 100 years, colleges and universities will still be playing football on Saturdays.

95

COLLEGE FOOTBALL'S WINNINGEST TEAMS

MICHIGAN WOLVERINES

SYRACUSE ORANGE

PITT PANTHERS

PENN STATE NITTANY LIONS

NOTRE DAME FIGHTING IRISH

OHIO STATE BUCKEYES

WEST VIRGINIA MOUNTAINEERS

NAVY MIDSHIPMEN

TENNESSEE VOLUNTEERS

VIRGINIA TECH HOKIES

ARKANSAS RAZORBACKS

GEORGIA TECH YELLOW JACKETS

CLEMSON TIGERS

GEORGIA BULLDOGS

ALABAMA CRIMSON TIDE

AUBURN TIGERS

TEXAS A&M AGGIES

FLORIDA GATORS

LSU TIGERS

Based on all-time wins through 2017.

TIMELINE

1869

The first organized college football game is played on November 6, with Rutgers beating Princeton by a score of 6–4.

1890

The Army Cadets and the Navy Midshipmen play their first football game on November 29, at West Point in New York. Navy, which established a team 11 years earlier, wins 24–0.

1902

The first Rose Bowl is played on January 1 in Pasadena, California. Michigan beats Stanford 49–0, a contest so lopsided that the game isn't staged again until 1916.

1916

Georgia Tech beats Cumberland University 222–0 on October 7, the largest margin of victory in college football history.

1936

The AP publishes its first national rankings compiled by sportswriters on October 19, with Minnesota, Duke, and Army taking the top three spots. The major poll era is launched.

1944

Army, led by running backs Doc Blanchard and Glenn Davis, finishes the season 9–0 to earn its first of two consecutive AP national championships, the only two for the Black Knights.

1953

CBS televises the Orange Bowl on January 1 to a national audience for the first time as Alabama beats Syracuse 61–6.

1968

Harvard and Yale finish in a 29–29 tie on November 23 in a game of unbeaten teams playing for the Ivy League championship. The headline in Harvard's student newspaper reads, "Harvard Beats Yale 29-29."

1971

Nebraska beats Oklahoma 35–31 on November 25 in a matchup of unbeaten Big Eight conference rivals billed as "The Game of the Century." Nebraska goes on to win the national championship after beating Alabama in the Orange Bowl.

1992

The Bowl Coalition debuts, increasing the likelihood that the top two teams in the country will play in a major bowl game. The Bowl Alliance replaces the Bowl Coalition in the 1995 season with a few tweaks.

1995

Illinois and Wisconsin finish at 3–3 on November 25, the last tie in a college football game. Overtime begins with the 1996 season.

1998

The BCS arrives, with the Rose Bowl included in the selection process for the first time. Tennessee, the No. 1 team, beats Florida State, ranked No. 2, in the consensus title game in the Fiesta Bowl.

2004

Instant replay arrives in college football, with the Big Ten experimenting with the use of video review of close calls at televised conference games.

2007

The BCS holds its first stand-alone title game after the traditional bowls, as Florida beats Ohio State 41–14 on January 8 in Glendale, Arizona.

2014

The last major wave of realignment takes effect on July 1, with 12 teams in the NCAA's Football Bowl Subdivision switching leagues.

2015

Ohio State wins the inaugural College Football Playoff, beating Oregon in the championship game on January 12. This comes after Ohio State defeats Alabama in the Sugar Bowl and Oregon tops Florida State in the Rose Bowl on New Year's Day.

2017

Western Michigan beats Buffalo 71–68 in seven overtimes in a Mid-American Conference game on October 7, the highest-scoring contest in modern NCAA FBS history.

2018

Alabama beats Georgia in overtime of the College Football Playoff championship on January 8, giving coach Nick Saban his sixth national title, five with the Crimson Tide. Saban matches his Alabama predecessor, Bear Bryant, with the most championships of the major poll era.

THE WINNERS

COLLEGE FOOTBALL'S WINNINGEST TEAMS

1. Michigan (944–340–36), .729
2. Notre Dame (908–324–42), .729
3. Yale (902–374–55), .698
4. Ohio State (900–324–53), .725
5. Texas (899–367–33), .705
6. Nebraska (893–381–40), .695
7. Alabama (893–328–43), .723
8. Oklahoma (886–323–53), .723
9. Penn State (880–387–41), .688

Through 2017 season, per NCAA.com. Schools need at least 25 years in the top division to be eligible. Due to record-keeping discrepancies, some schools report different records.

MOST NATIONAL CHAMPIONSHIPS, BY ASSOCIATED PRESS POLL SINCE 1936

1. Alabama, 11
2. Notre Dame, 8
3T. Oklahoma, 7
3T. USC, 7
5. Ohio State, 6

MOST NATIONAL CHAMPIONSHIPS, SINCE BCS ERA BEGAN IN 1998

1. Alabama, 5
2T. Florida, 2
2T. Florida State, 2
2T. LSU, 2
2T. Ohio State, 2

THE RECORDS

MOST PASSING YARDS IN A GAME

734, Connor Halliday, Washington State (vs. Cal), October 4, 2014

734, Patrick Mahomes, Texas Tech (vs. Oklahoma), October 22, 2016

MOST RECEIVING YARDS IN A GAME

405, Troy Edwards, Louisiana Tech (vs. Nebraska), August 29, 1998

MOST RUSHING YARDS IN A GAME

427, Samaje Perine, Oklahoma (vs. Kansas), November 22, 2014

MOST PASSING TOUCHDOWNS IN A GAME

11, David Klingler, Houston (vs. Eastern Washington), November 17, 1990

MOST RECEIVING TOUCHDOWNS IN A GAME

7, Rashaun Woods, Oklahoma State (vs. SMU), September 20, 2003

MOST RUSHING TOUCHDOWNS IN A GAME
8, Howard Griffith, Illinois (vs. Southern Illinois), September 22, 1990

MOST PASSING YARDS IN A SEASON
5,833, B. J. Symons, Texas Tech, 2003

MOST RECEIVING YARDS IN A SEASON
2,060, Trevor Insley, Nevada, 1999

MOST RUSHING YARDS IN A SEASON
2,628, Barry Sanders, Oklahoma State, 1988

MOST PASSING TOUCHDOWNS IN A SEASON
58, Colt Brennan, Hawaii, 2006

MOST RECEIVING TOUCHDOWNS IN A SEASON
27, Troy Edwards, Louisiana Tech, 1998

MOST RUSHING TOUCHDOWNS IN A SEASON
37, Barry Sanders, Oklahoma State, 1988

Accurate through the 2017 season.

FOR MORE INFORMATION

BOOKS

The Editors of Sports Illustrated. *Sports Illustrated: The College Football Book.* New York: Sports Illustrated Books, 2008.

Layden, Tim. *Blood, Sweat and Chalk: The Ultimate Football Playbook: How the Great Coaches Built Today's Game.* New York: Sports Illustrated Books, 2010.

MacCambridge, Michael, and Dan Jenkins. *ESPN College Football Encyclopedia.* New York: ESPN Books, 2005.

Stewart, Alva W. *College Football Stadiums.* Jefferson, NC: McFarland and Company, 2000.

ON THE WEB

AP Poll: All-Time
collegefootball.ap.org/ap-poll-all-time

The Heisman Trophy
www.heisman.com

Sports Reference: College Football
www.sports-reference.com/cfb

PLACES TO VISIT

COLLEGE FOOTBALL HALL OF FAME

250 Marietta St. NW
Atlanta, GA 30313
404-880-4800
www.cfbhall.com

This hall of fame and museum, founded in 1951, highlights the greatest players, coaches, and moments in the history of college football. The building used to be located in Ohio and then Indiana before reopening in Georgia in 2014.

NCAA HALL OF CHAMPIONS

700 W. Washington St.
Indianapolis, IN 46204
317-916-4255
www.ncaahallofchampions.org

This interactive museum at the NCAA's headquarters features all 23 sanctioned college sports and includes trivia challenges, team rankings, video highlights, and various artifacts from the history of the games, plus virtual reality sports simulators.

SELECT BIBLIOGRAPHY

BOOKS

Eisenhammer, Fred, and Eric Sondheimer. *College Football's Most Memorable Games, 1913 through 1990: The Stories of 54 History-Making Contests.* Jefferson, NC: McFarland and Company, 1992.

Gitlin, Marty. *The Greatest College Football Rivalries of All Time: The Civil War, the Iron Bowl, and Other Memorable Matchups.* Lanham, MD: Rowman and Littlefield, 2014.

Ours, Robert. *Bowl Games: College Football's Greatest Tradition.* Yardley, PA: Westholme Publishing, 2004.

Weinreb, Michael. *Season of Saturdays: A History of College Football in 14 Games.* New York: Simon and Schuster, 2014.

ONLINE

Hennes, Doug. "O'Shaughnessy, St. Thomas, and the Bond of Loyalty." *University of St. Thomas*, 3 Jan. 2007, www.news.stthomas.edu/oshaughnessy-st-thomas-and-the-bond-of-loyalty/.

Martin, Tim. "40 Years Later, ND-Michigan State Tie Still One for Ages," Associated Press, 20 Sept. 2006, www.newsok.com/article/2850685/game-of-century-still-reverberates?.

Nack, William. "A Life Cut Short," *Sports Illustrated*, 4 Sept. 1989, www.si.com/vault/1989/09/04/106780587/a-life-cut-short.

Rittenberg, Adam. "How the Playoff Came to Be," *ESPN.com*, 10 Dec. 2014, www.espn.com/college-football/story/_/id/12002638/an-oral-history-college-football-playoff.

INDEX

ABOUT THE AUTHOR

Dave Campbell has been a sportswriter for the Associated Press since 2000, reporting on the major Minnesota teams and writing other national stories for the worldwide wire service. Born in Illinois, raised in Wisconsin, settled in Minnesota, and married to a Michigan State graduate, he has spent a lifetime closely following college football, especially the Big Ten. He has a degree in print journalism from the University of St. Thomas in St. Paul, Minnesota, and he lives in Minneapolis with his wife, son, and daughter.